WOODCUT

WOODCUT

BRYAN NASH GILL

Introduction by **Bill McKibben**

PA PRESS

PRINCETON ARCHITECTURAL PRESS · NEW YORK

I DEDICATE THIS BOOK TO MY SON,

FOREST NASH GILL. May you thrive like a mighty oak.

PUBLISHED BY
PRINCETON ARCHITECTURAL PRESS
A DIVISION OF CHRONICLE BOOKS LLC
70 WEST 36TH STREET
NEW YORK, NY 10018
PAPRESS.COM

PRINTED AND BOUND IN CHINA
27 26 25 24   4 3 2 1
UPDATED EDITION

ISBN 978-1-7972-3268-3

EDITOR, UPDATED EDITION: JENNIFER N. THOMPSON
DESIGNERS: DEB WOOD & PAUL WAGNER

IMAGE CREDITS
ALL PHOTOGRAPHY BY PHILLIP FORTUNE
UNLESS OTHERWISE NOTED.
SARA BADER: 106–9, 110 (BOTTOM), 111–19
BRYAN NASH GILL: 28
ALLEN PHILLIPS: 21, 110 (TOP)

PP. 1–5, 121–23: DETAILS FROM WILLOW, 2011.
FOR FULL PRINT, SEE PAGE 65.
PP. 6–8: DETAILS FROM LEADER, 2010.
FOR FULL PRINT, SEE PAGE 39.
PP. 124–28: DETAILS FROM SOUTHPORT OAK, 2009,
AND SOUTHPORT OAK, 2010.
FOR FULL PRINTS, SEE PAGES 46–47.

LIBRARY OF CONGRESS CONTROL NUMBER: 2024935107
THE LIBRARY OF CONGRESS HAS CATALOGED THE PREVIOUS
EDITION UNDER ISBN 978-1-61689-048-3.

CONTENTS

BILL
MCKIBBEN

Looking at these wonderful prints brought two things immediately to mind.

The first was the series of crosscuts I've seen over the years, often at groves of enormous sequoias or in local history museums, that show the passage of time in tree rings. If the felled or fallen tree was old enough, the small flags placed on the rings would go back to Shakespeare's plays, or Newton's apple, or perhaps before: moments marked in a somehow reassuring record of our past, demonstrating that the turmoil of whatever epoch we found ourselves in belonged, fairly smoothly, with what had come before. The record of the passing of time, preserved in tree rings, was calmer than the record preserved in history books; the human passions, sometimes violent, were evened out in the placid record of the forest.

The second was a news story that ran in the *Washington Post* late in 2023 about a dendrochronologist, Kiyomi Morino, who has been studying ponderosa pines in the high Sonoran Desert for many years. At the University of Arizona lab known as the center of tree-ring science, Morino had access to "the world's largest collection of tree samples: massive cross sections of giant sequoias, pencil-shaped cores taken from stalwart Alaskan pines, roof beams of historic buildings, charcoal from fires that burned out long ago." They showed the droughts and floods and heat waves and cold snaps of the millennia. And then they showed 2023, which was the hottest year, scientists told us, of at least the last 125,000. That is to say, we lived through—are living through—a climatic disruption far greater than any living tree (or anything we'd recognize as a human society) has ever endured. And it's showing. When Morino looked, for example, at a tree labeled Bigelow 224, the tree's "most recent growth appeared in vivid, violet detail on an adjacent computer screen. The rings from 2021 and 2022 looked relatively normal: Each was dozens of cells wide, with a robust strip of dense latewood.

But this year's ring was less than a third of the size of the others, and it hardly contained any latewood." Apparently, "the record heat and delayed rainfall have stressed the trees so much that they stopped growing in the middle of the year," something that appeared nowhere else in the record.

What I'm trying to say is that these remarkable woodcut prints have a poignancy that goes beyond their beauty. They not only show the remarkable adaptations of individual organisms— all those burls that indicate some infestation or deadfall—but also preserve a record of normality, from what we are now forced to think of as a "before time," back when, just a few years ago, the world was operating with something like its old and familiar cadences and rhythms. We've broken that record now, and not in a good sense— that is, the record itself now will show not the relatively smooth passage of time but the sudden evidence of the most dramatic thing human beings have ever done, which is to change the composition of the atmosphere and hence the temperature of the Earth.

And so we have these remarkable images from from the late Bryan Nash Gill (1961–2013), which of course also summon up the Rorschach inkblots that psychiatrists have used for generations to start people illuminating the inner workings of their minds. But Gill's images force us to examine our relationships not with our fathers or our spouses or ourselves, but with our societies and civilizations.

The forests from which these trees are taken have lived with humans for a long time now. Those of us who have made our lives in the woods—in my case the birch-beech-maple hardwoods and the spruce-hemlock conifers of the mountainous Northeast—know that we've taken an unforgiving toll on those groves; there is very little "old growth" left. But we also know that humans can take a step back and let the forest rebuild. The Adirondacks, the woods I know best, are a literal second-chance Eden, once clear-cut stem to stern but now a kind of botanical paradise, where you need to be a pretty good forester to know you're not in virgin forest.

And if that's true of the collective, it's also true of the individual specimen. The resilience of trees, I think, is what these images celebrate above all—that, like humans, they can take a punch, perhaps bend or twist, and yet keep on, inexorably. The force of life runs through them with calm but undeniable resolve.

I don't know if that story is over now—I fear that in many places it may be. The great rainforests of the Amazon seem to be turning to savanna in real time; the boreal forests of Canada and Siberia burned last year in a conflagration that sent endless clouds of smoke pouring south (and enormous invisible clouds of carbon dioxide into the air, a vicious feedback loop that augurs more trouble to come). But if so, all the more reason to be deeply grateful for this record of struggle and quiet triumph.

Trees—and we are a planet of trees even more than of people— are unaccountably beautiful. I love them in every aspect—the early, light spring brightness, the deep, leathery late summer green, the orgasm of color that comes to my latitudes, and the bare stickness that arrives in mid-October and lasts the winter through. But now we know, thanks to this remarkable artist, how lovely and haunting they are at the heart as well. It's a gift for the moment, and for the ages.

BRYAN
NASH GILL

I grew up on a farm in the northwest corner of Connecticut. The natural beauty of the earth and its plants and creatures were the backdrop of my formative years. Early on, I learned to experiment, improvise, and get the most out of what was available. The work of farming yielded hard-earned, tangible results.

In addition to the usual childhood playthings, I was surrounded by and constantly using the tools I found in the barn and elsewhere on the farm. I used these instruments in practical and creative ways while exploring my environment. The woods were my playground and place to find building materials. My brother and I constructed forts and lean-to villages and rerouted streams in order to make waterfalls and homes for the crawfish we caught. The nature around us displayed beautiful and complex qualities. Pattern, texture, and color were everywhere. This sense of discovery has been a governing force throughout my life.

In graduate school, I concluded that art is (or should be) an experience that brings you closer to understanding yourself in relation to your surroundings. This simple insight has had a profound effect on me. When I returned to my family's land in Connecticut, I felt a connection between my creative process and the natural environment in which I was raised. Coming home gave me the comfort and confidence to reconnect with the place I explored as a child. I started looking at the land in a new way in order to better understand it, and myself. Older, and with more patience, I would walk just to walk, stopping to look and listen. I found enjoyment in simply being in the woods. This newfound relationship to nature directly influenced my work.

In 1998, I began building a studio adjacent to my home. I also enrolled in my first etching class, taught by Anthony Kirk at the Center for Contemporary Printmaking in Norwalk, Connecticut. I created my first relief print out of a piece of wood salvaged from the construction of my studio, which was built out of pine and hemlock from my property. During the building process, I became captivated by the end grain of lumber—the undulations, texture, and shades of parallel lines found on a single block of wood. I had to print it.

My lumber explorations progressed to tree prints. The logs that I cut and split and used for heating my house and studio, or for building a fence, were also perfect for printing. They were beautiful in their own right. So much was revealed in the cut— looking inside the tree, I discovered its history and character, and then printed it. Pure in concept and execution, but complex and intricate in pattern, these one-to-one, large-scale relief prints capture the essence of the woodblocks. They document the nature I see around me.

TREES

In printmaking terms, these woodcuts are defined as relief prints; they are impressions of the raised grain of the wood. The woodblocks used to create the prints are cross sections— through trunks, near roots to branches—of diverse species of trees, including ash, cedar, locust, maple, oak, pine, spruce, and willow. The blocks range in scale (one of the largest, *Ash*, is approximately four feet in diameter) and age (*Cedar Pole*, from an unassuming telephone pole, is over two hundred years old). Many of the blocks were foraged from local lumberyards, others were scavenged from property surrounding the studio or neighboring land, and *Southport Oak* came from a stately tree at the Pequot Library in Southport, Connecticut. Each cut reveals a unique story through shape, pattern, color, and various irregularities (such as the small metal spike wedged deep in the block of *Spruce*). These characteristics are transferred from tree to paper in alarming detail—capturing every ring, line, crack, and other natural and process-related marks.

ASH, 2003

49¾ × 46¼ INCHES

This was the first relief print I created from
a tree cut. When I pulled the print, I was surprised
and inspired by how well the details of the block
transferred to the paper. The outline is sharp
and the growth rings are discrete. Also present
are checks, or cracks, from the curing of the block
and several marks from cutting and sanding
the surface (evident in the top center of the print).

82 YEARS PRINTED

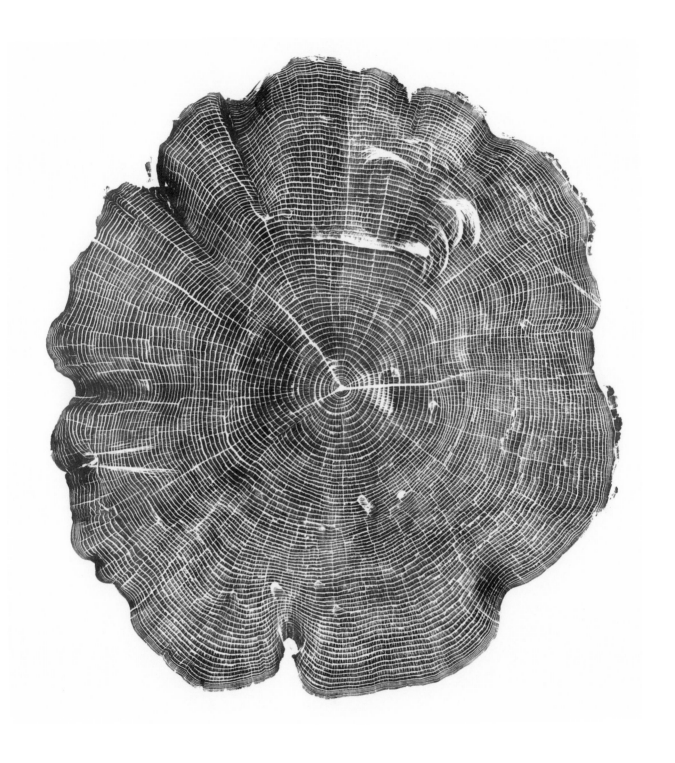

RED ASH, 2007

49¾ × 46¼ INCHES

*Printing in red ink was an investigation that
proved to be an exciting variation of the original—
it is simple but impactful and brings an unexpected
richness to the reading.*

82 YEARS PRINTED

HEARTWOOD, 2007

ASH, 12 × 9¾ INCHES

The heartwood is the central, nonliving part of the trunk with the densest and hardest wood. This is a full bleed print of the center of the Ash *block—the annual rings radiate from the tree's first year at the center to the edges of the paper.*

25 YEARS PRINTED

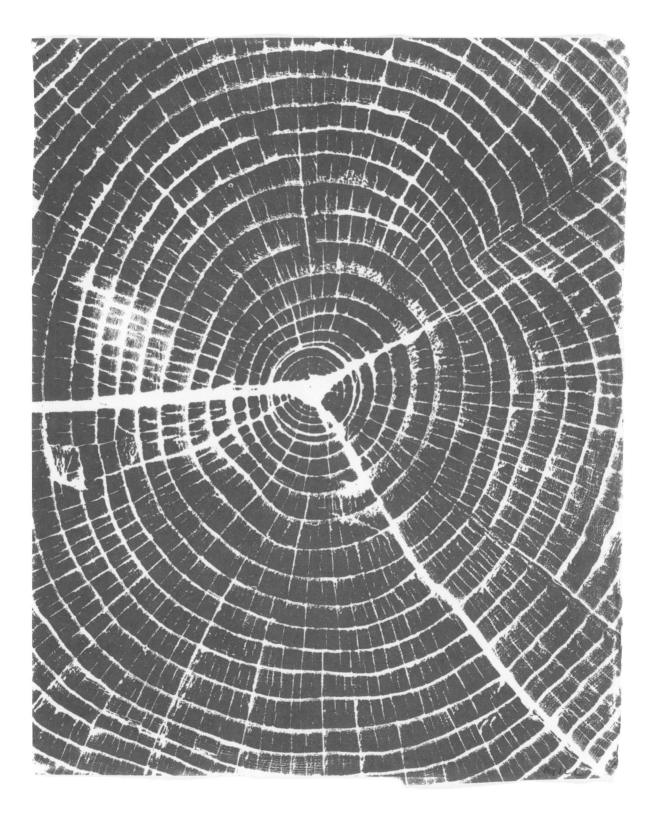

BLACK LOCUST SERIES, 2003

11¾ × 11 INCHES, EACH

An early experiment in relief printing, this series explores the application and saturation of ink and other solvents. Additionally, each image was printed during a distinct stage of the sanding process and the sequence documents the slowly diminishing marks of the chain saw. With varying treatments, the same block produces three unique results.

64 YEARS PRINTED

HEMLOCK 82, 2008
39½ × 38¼ INCHES

This trunk was found at a pig farm in Barkhamsted, Connecticut. I was immediately drawn to the strong pattern of the wavy rings (the result of irregularities in the growth of the bole). In the print, a cut branch creates a prominent form that extends from the center to the right edge, and various insect holes dot the lower perimeter of the block. (See pages 113 and 116.)

82 YEARS PRINTED

HEMLOCK 82, 2008
39½ × 38¼ INCHES

A large check defines this edition of Hemlock 82. *As with all blocks, the wood changes over time—with varying conditions of heat and moisture, and even insect activity (note the additional holes throughout). The orientation of the block on the paper also has shifted, further distinguishing this print from the original.*

82 YEARS PRINTED

SPRUCE, 2008
NORWAY SPRUCE, 40¾ × 37½ INCHES

Once the emperor of my neighbor's property, this tree served as a lightning rod to thwart otherwise direct hits to the house. When the tree was twenty years old, a low-lying branch was cut, and at thirty, a metal spike was driven into its body. As one of the softer woods, spruce is susceptible to insect invasion, shown here as white tunneling trails. This print was created with multiple layers of colors, applied wet on wet— a technique to simulate the depth and complexities of the natural block. (See woodblock on page 119.)

97 YEARS PRINTED

DOUBLE CRESCENT, 2009

NORWAY SPRUCE, 27 × 12¼ INCHES, EACH HALF

One block was used to make this image. This wood is from the same lightning tree as Spruce, *but is a section from farther up the trunk. Notice the branch that was cut by hand then healed by the tree.*

45 YEARS PRINTED

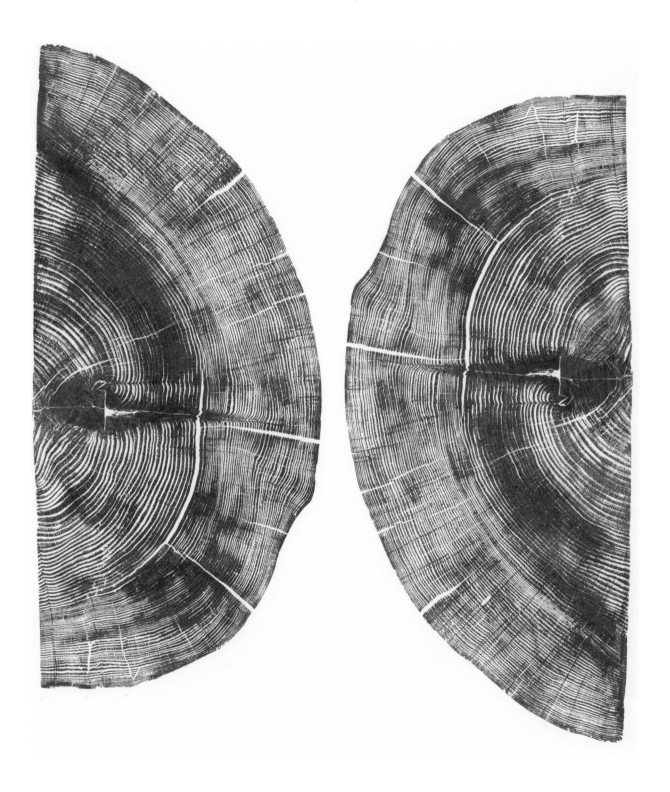

PICEA ABIES, 2011

NORWAY SPRUCE, CLOTH, 40¾ × 37½ INCHES

This print was created with the opposing surface of the Spruce block. Using cloth produced a dense, yet dimensional result. The multilayered process involved printing in black, then applying turpentine to soften the outer edge and imply a sense of movement (evident in the space of the check). Finally, the center of the block was overprinted with white ink. The finished piece has remarkable depth and an otherworldly quality. (See woodblock on page 119.)

97 YEARS PRINTED

BLACK LOCUST WITH *BARK,* 2009

20 × 19¼ INCHES

The bark is the defining characteristic of this piece.
When printed, the deep furrows form a saw blade–like
image. The parallel lines in the upper left are likely
the result of an insect invasion; graphically, they act
as a pointer to the double center.

87 YEARS PRINTED

LEADER, 2009

ASH, 30½ × 21½ INCHES

In this oblong section, the leader, or trunk, is dividing into two. The cores, surrounded by rings, create a topographical feel. A rotted branch, which was healed over in the final years of growth, is encapsulated in the lower right of the print, and at the center, remnants of bark can be found in the space between the leaders.

80 YEARS PRINTED

LEADER, 2010

ASH, 30½ × 21½ INCHES

As the wood is allowed to dry naturally, it expands and contracts. The newly checked block was printed, documenting one of the drying phases. These cracks reveal spatial shifts over time.

80 YEARS PRINTED

LEADER, 2011

ASH, CLOTH, 30½ × 21½ INCHES

Printing on cotton cloth produces dynamic results and has opened up a new direction in my relief printing. The ability to apply many colors and media adds depth to the prints, pulling out new characteristics from the blocks of wood. In this piece, a mix of ink and solvent creates a soft, three-dimensional quality.

80 YEARS PRINTED

LOCUST, 2009

18 × 15½ INCHES

*I discovered this block while cutting split-rail
fencing. The print showcases the distinct separation
of heartwood from sapwood (the softer, productive
layers of wood), as well as the beginning of
branching and a raylike pattern of checks.*

67 YEARS PRINTED

MAPLE, 2009

RED MAPLE, 23¼ × 15¾ INCHES

As I was preparing firewood for the winter,
I noticed the undulating outer edge of this maple
specimen. Maples generally grow straight and
tall in the thick woods; however, at ground level,
some take on a naturally curvy shape. Lacking
visible growth rings (typical of hard maple wood),
the perimeter is imperative to the success of the
print. The block also features marks of peeling bark
and rot, seen in the white shapes just off center.
(See woodblock on page 109.)

79 YEARS PRINTED

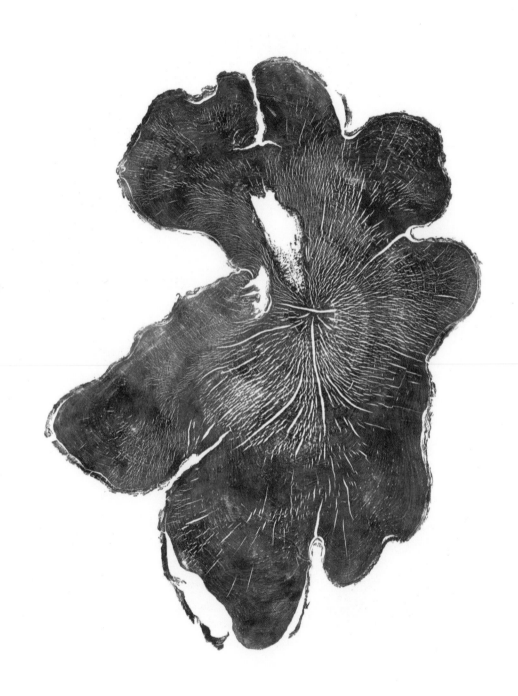

SOUTHPORT OAK, 2009
WHITE OAK, 32½ × 31½ INCHES

This tree was planted by the founders of the Pequot Library in Southport, Connecticut, over a hundred years ago and was harvested in 2009. White oak is a hardwood that has an exceptional lifespan in the right conditions. In this print, the even spacing of annual rings is indicative of a consistent growth environment. This section also shows that the tree was pruned in its twenty-eighth year.

109 YEARS PRINTED

SOUTHPORT OAK, 2010
WHITE OAK, 32½ × 31½ INCHES

After the first printing, the block was left to air dry in the studio, allowing it to check. Oak will always check unless it is kiln dried. Here, the block is nearly split into several pieces, making it fragile and difficult to print.

109 YEARS PRINTED

HONEY LOCUST, 2010
19½ × 19¼ INCHES

With its peculiar shape and furrowed bark, this tree clearly stood out from the stack of logs it was found in. The white "T" form on the bottom left of the print began as a bark pocket, caused by the undulating cambium layer growing around and encapsulating the bark. Moisture in the pocket attracted carpenter ants, which excavated the inner deadwood.

31 YEARS PRINTED

CEDAR POLE, 2011

23½ × 22⅛ INCHES

An arborist friend brought me this cut telephone pole. We were intrigued by the extremely tight growth rings. From start to finish, it was very challenging to print this piece. Every step—from raising the grain to applying the ink to pressing and printing the contours—had to be meticulous in order to clearly read each ring.

200+ YEARS PRINTED

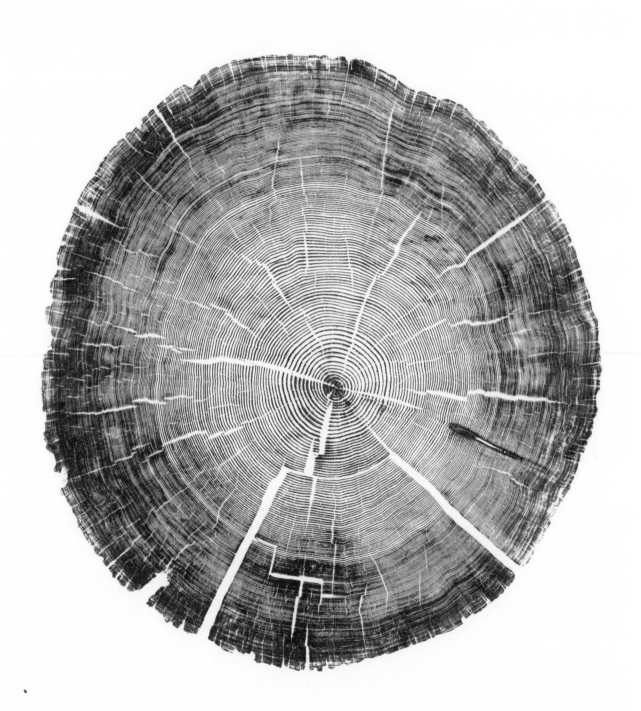

COMPRESSION WOOD, 2011

RED OAK, 20 × 19½ INCHES

The term compression wood *describes trees that grow abnormally in the forest. This growth may result from heavy snow or uprooting, or simply from the tree reaching for sunlight. The seashell-like pattern of this block implies that the tree was bending in the direction of the top of the print.*

76 YEARS PRINTED

CRESCENT, 2011

EASTERN WHITE PINE, 23 × 19 INCHES

The pith in some softwoods rots while the
cambium and sapwood layers are still vital
and the tree remains standing. In this instance,
the tree survived a trauma, the open wound
slowly healed, then rot set in and carpenter
ants infiltrated the space, creating a hollow.

45 YEARS PRINTED

MAPLE LARGE, 2011
SUGAR MAPLE, 41 × 51½ INCHES

There are several boneyards where I go to scout cut trees. The massiveness of this sugar maple (over four feet wide) was my initial fascination. During the drying process, the large, sloping line created by my chain saw was closed in by the shrinking wood. In proximity to this line, I left additional cut marks that typically are sanded away before printing.

AGE NOT DETERMINED

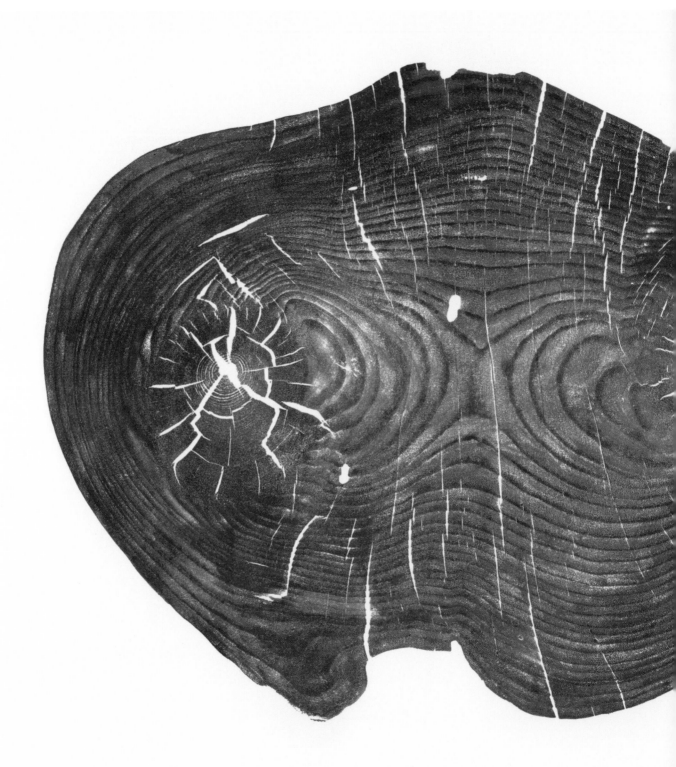

PINE BRANCH, 2011

EASTERN WHITE PINE, 14½ × 19¼ INCHES

An investigation into directional cuts, this block is from the edge of the tree, perpendicular to the trunk, where two branches extend out. The shape of the block and the spacing of the branches give this print an anthropomorphic quality. (See woodblock on page 109.)

29 YEARS PRINTED

FOLLOWING SPREAD

PINE I, 2011

EASTERN WHITE PINE, 30½ × 28½ INCHES

The asymmetrical shape of this pine strays from the generic circular bole. This block is still green, saturated with water and sap. Set on a waxy, brown paper, the print captures this stage of freshness.

56 YEARS PRINTED

PINE II, 2011

EASTERN WHITE PINE, 27½ × 30 INCHES

After the block had time to cure, the surface of the wood was reworked. Removing the oozing sap and sanding the drier block further separated the springwood from the summerwood. This technique helped to create a cleaner print that is truer to the natural growth of the tree. The result, rotated almost 180 degrees from the first edition, has a vortexlike feel.

56 YEARS PRINTED

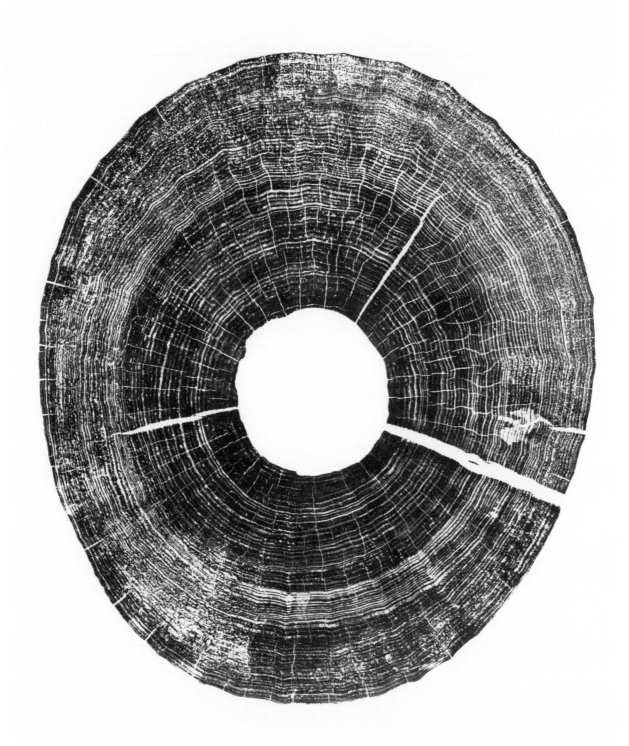

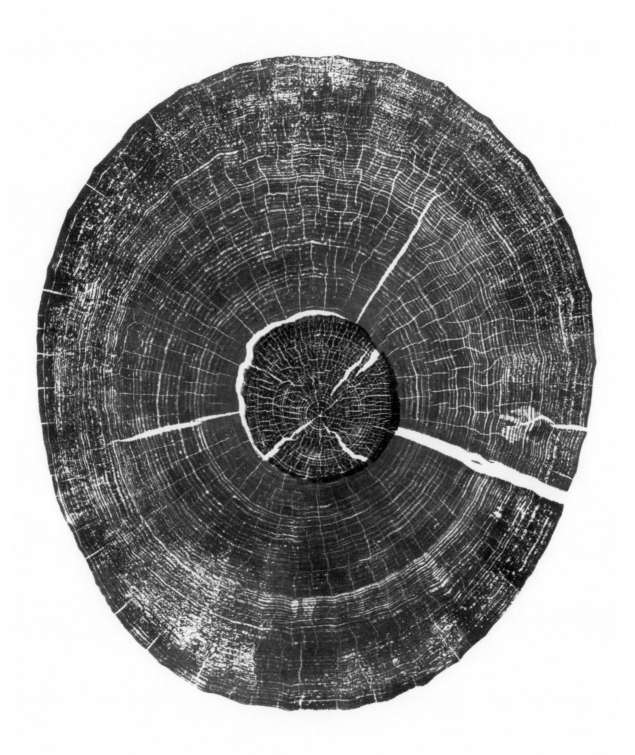

PIPE ROT, 2011
ASH, 29½ × 26 INCHES

This block was found at a local lumber mill. At thirty-two years old, the tree experienced a trauma, causing that year's growth ring to separate from the following year's growth. This allowed the center to be removed from the block of wood. This print also showcases the differentiation between the heartwood that encircles the void and the surrounding lighter sapwood.

66 YEARS PRINTED

PIPE ROT WITH *CENTER,* 2011
ASH, 29½ × 26 INCHES

After removing the core, the block of wood dried and the center no longer fit back into place. This dynamic is emphasized through the overprinted center, sitting on the full block.

66 YEARS PRINTED

WILLOW, 2011
WEEPING WILLOW, 36½ × 31 INCHES

This specimen was harvested from the bole just below the main leaders, where the pith splits into two. Willow grows relatively quickly in favorable conditions, evident in the loose growth rings. On the bottom edge, the irregular pattern is the result of a burgeoning burl.

51 YEARS PRINTED

EASTERN RED CEDAR, 2011

18¼ × 16½ INCHES

Red cedar is often used for fence posts because of its resistance to rot (it has a high oil content and is very dense). It also has an attractive purple center and a distinct, familiar smell that repels insects. This piece has a strong outer edge and when found had a vine of poison ivy growing up its bark. The print was created during the making of this book. (See page 115.)

77 YEARS PRINTED

LUMBER

The following prints are made from blocks of manufactured timber—including dimensional lumber, such as two-by-fours and four-by-fours, and plywood and other boards. These everyday building materials are prized for their machined standardization, yet they are often overlooked for their inherent beauty. Through the stacking of end grains (demonstrated in the basic form of *Four Square II*) or layering of face planes (represented in the colors of *Overlapping Planks*), rich patterns and prints emerge in simple rectilinear configurations.

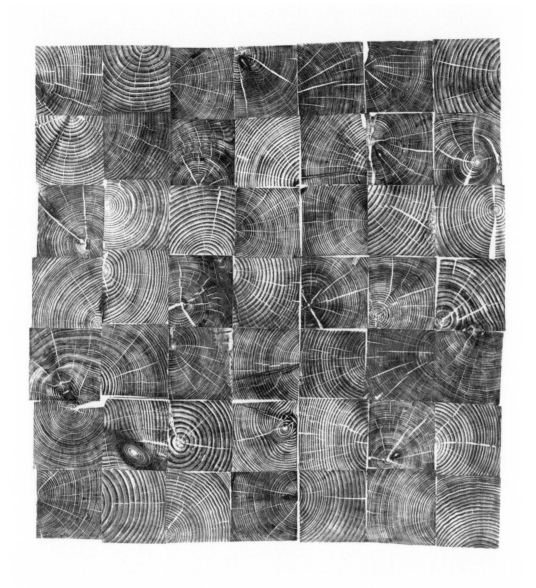

SCULPTURE PRINT I, 2010

42¼ × 37½ INCHES

CANT I, 2010

18¾ × 19¼ INCHES

FOUR SQUARE II, 2011

19¾ × 20½ INCHES

This image was printed four times from
a single block of wood. Before each printing,
the block was re-inked and repositioned.
The resulting composition creates a new
collective whole.

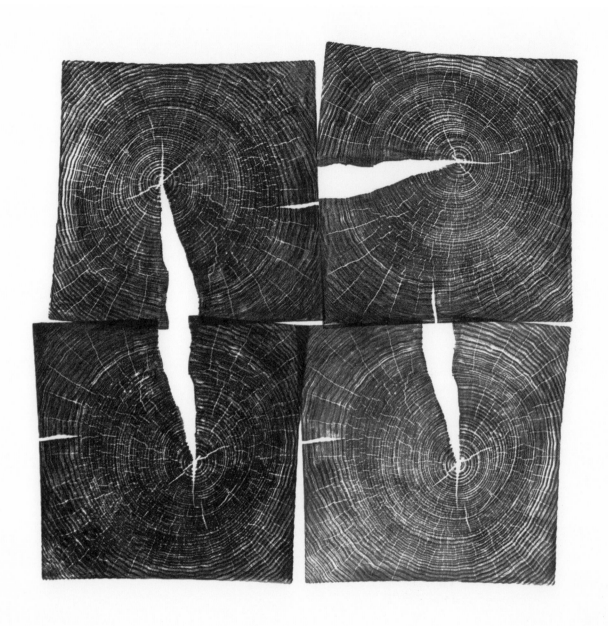

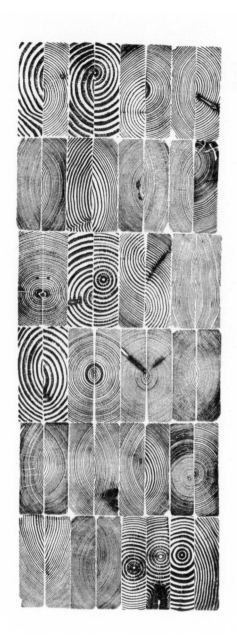

STACK I, 2011

32¾ × 12⅛ INCHES

STACK II, 2011

CLOTH, 32 × 24 INCHES

GLUE LAM, 2003

13¾ × 17¾ INCHES

This was one of the first prints I created from dimensional lumber. Glued laminated timber (a highly engineered material in which layers of timber are bonded together) is known for its superior structural strength and used as columns or beams. This print, made from two boards stacked and rotated, showcases the grain patterns of the glued lumber.

PLYWOOD I, 2004

8 × 5½ INCHES

Plywood is often made from glued sheets of wood
or veneer that are cut on the longitudinal axis,
parallel to the pith. By printing the surface
of the plywood, the typically understated pattern
is pulled out of the utilitarian material.

1/1   PLYWOOD I   Miil '04

INTERIOR, 2003

9¼ × 6 INCHES

OVERLAPPING PLANKS, 2007

19⅞ × 18¾ INCHES

PINE PLANK I, 2011

18 × 64 INCHES

CEDAR STACK III, 2011

16½ × 24 INCHES

CEDAR STACK IV, 2011

24 × 16½ INCHES

OFFCUTS

Beyond the scope and scale of the tree cross sections, these cuts expose the fascinating characteristics of knots, burls, and branches, as well as rot and insect invasion. From the perforated scrub of *Heart Pine* to the deep cut of *Spike Knot* to the various bookmatch burl explorations, each print makes a distinct impression. A majority of the works feature burls, outgrowths that result from a fungus, virus, or other stress and that are celebrated in woodworking for their swirling patterns. These remarkable designs are picked up in the relief prints, culminating in *Rolling Burl*, a 360-degree recording of a burl that encircles an entire tree trunk.

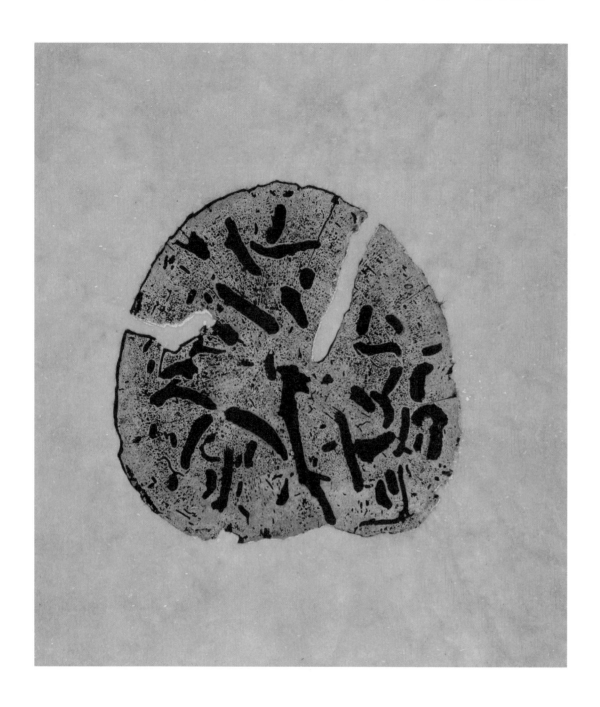

HEART PINE, 2011
SOUTHERN LONGLEAF PINE, 11 × 11 INCHES

SPIKE KNOT, 2006
EASTERN WHITE PINE, 30 × 22⅜ INCHES

CEDAR BURL, 2011

21 × 15½ INCHES

This is the first burl that I successfully printed.
The juxtaposition of geometric and irregular
shapes creates a compelling composition.
In the cross section, the intricate dendrite forms
of the growth are revealed. Also evident is the
deterioration of annual rings as the burl spreads
and pushes out of the bole.

APPLE BURL, 2011

11⅛ × 15¾ INCHES

This burl came from a local apple orchard.
The block was created by cutting the burl
longitudinally down the middle and placing
the cut parts side by side, similar to
a woodworker's technique of bookmatching,
to achieve a mirror image–like result.

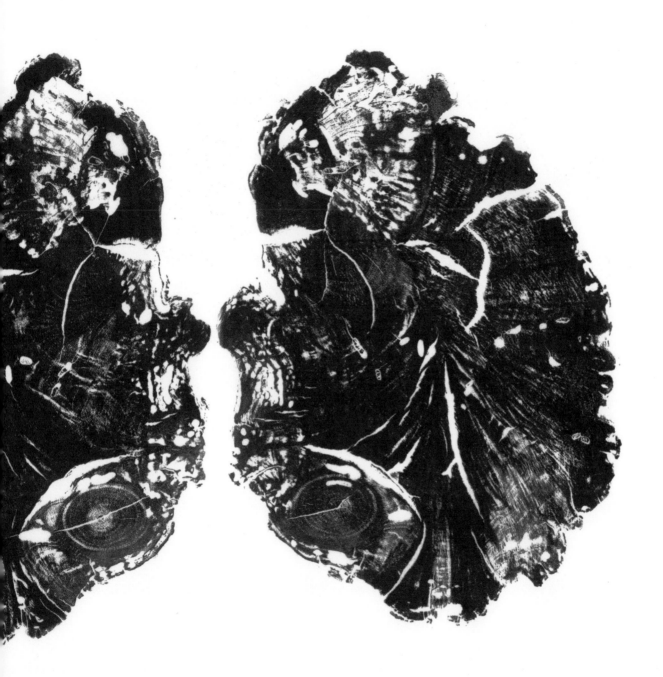

BOOKMATCH I, 2011

10½ × 17¾ INCHES

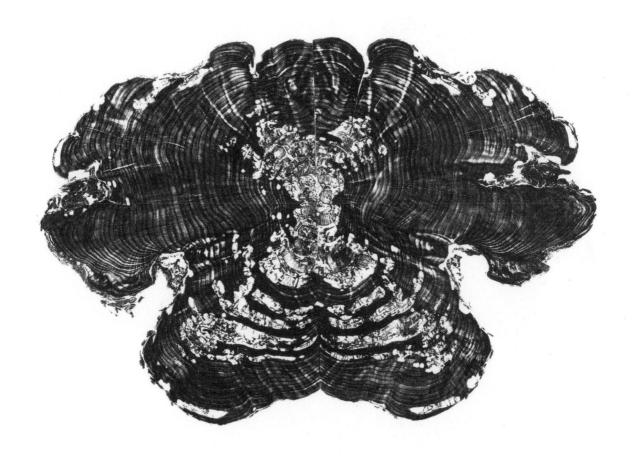

BOOKMATCH II, 2011

15¾ × 23¾ INCHES

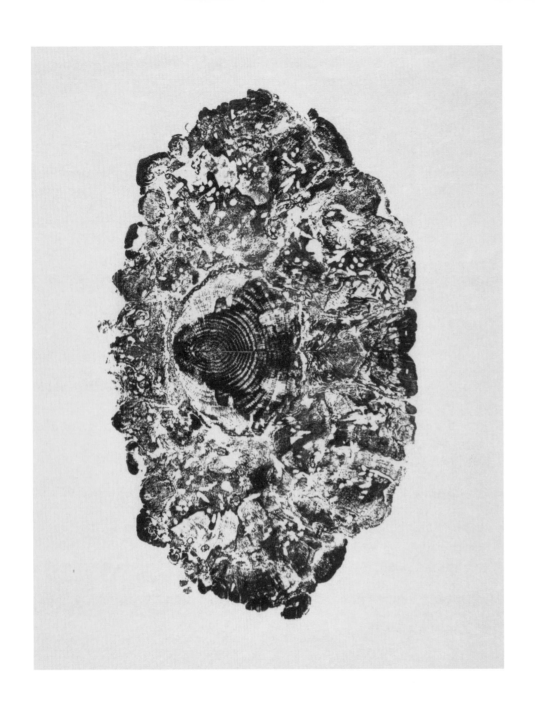

BOOKMATCH III, 2011

22½ × 14¼ INCHES

BOOKMATCH IV, 2011
19 × 14 INCHES

YEW I, 2000

13 × 8¾ INCHES

YEW II, 2000

13 × 8¾ INCHES

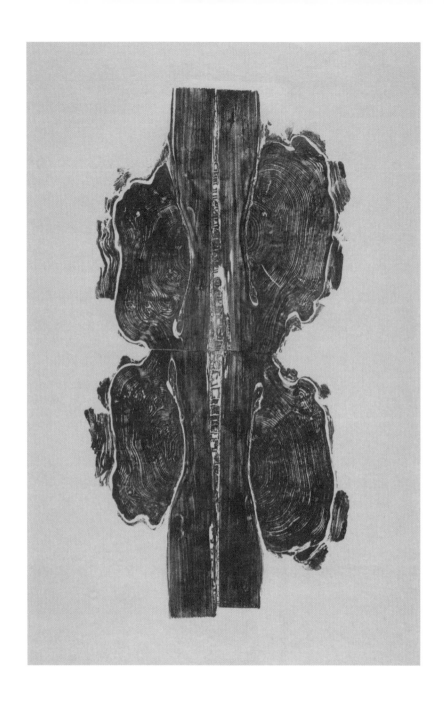

DOUBLE BOOKMATCH I, 2011

26 × 13½ INCHES

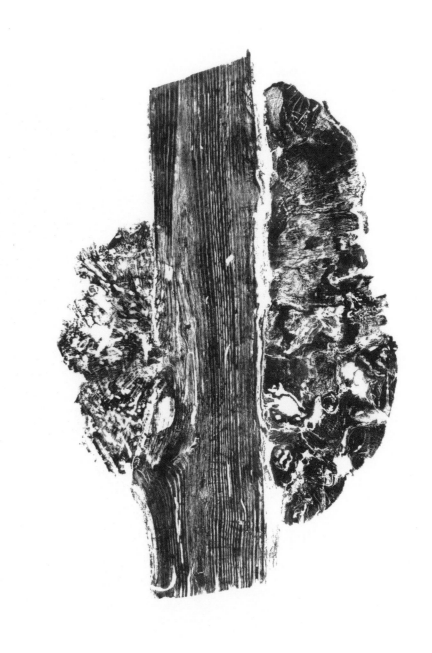

WHITE OAK BURL I, 2011

26¾ × 17 INCHES

CEDAR BRANCH, 2011

13½ × 13¾ INCHES

In this print, branches are extending out of a burl-infected tree. The mix of patterns, from branches and burl, creates a knotlike form. The origin of the virus can be seen in the triangle shape near the center of the print.

FOLLOWING SPREAD

ROLLING BURL I, 2011

14 × 40 INCHES

The longitudinal surface is any plane that runs parallel to the pith. This print is of the circumference of a tree, specifically the outer edge of an encompassing burl. It was achieved by squaring the outside of the burl, creating four distinct surfaces to be rolled and printed consecutively. (See woodblock on page 109.)

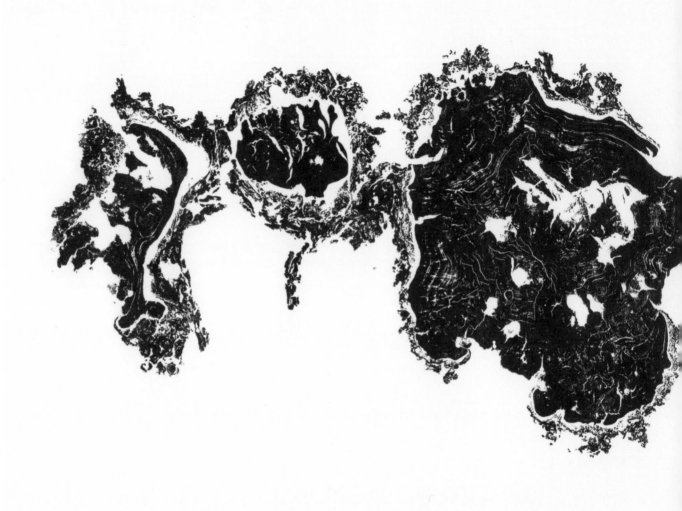

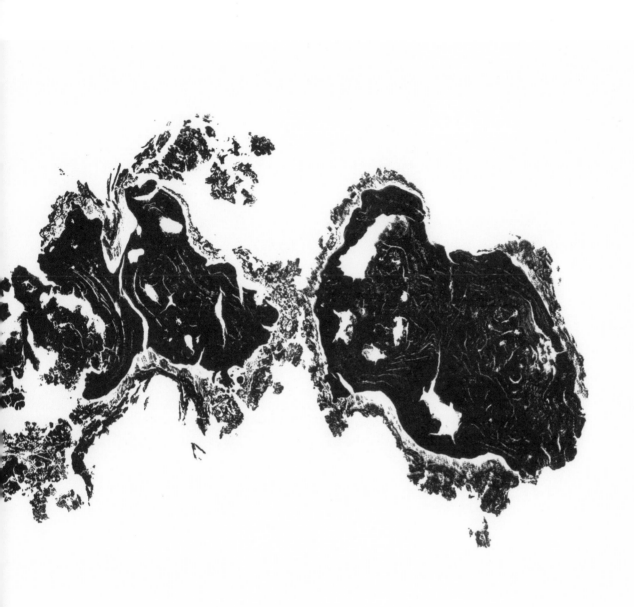

ON PROCESS
AND DISCOVERY

Breezeway connecting house
and studio

Bryan Nash Gill discusses his printmaking beginnings, process, and
plans. Here, he describes his involved approach, step by step, revealing
the labor and nuances in making each print.

FIRST PRINTS

The lumber prints were my first relief prints. Wood has inherently
beautiful surfaces. The traditional woodcut is carved into the
surface of flat birch plywood. Rather than remove material to
create an image, in my prints, I have tried to keep true to the wood,
exposing its natural (or in the case of lumber, its manufactured)
characteristics. For example, I printed *Plywood I* [*p.79*] because of
those parallel curvy, wavy lines.

When building my studio, I started looking at the end grain
of two-by-fours, four-by-fours, and eight-by-eights. I thought,
I bet those could print—that was the first investigation. From
there, I began stacking the lumber. I've always been into stacking
and piling. Stacking is more of a human endeavor, a manmade
endeavor; we stack our books, we stack our clothes—we don't pile
them. Piling is a more organic stacking. Leaves pile up on each
other. The debris in the woods piles up and creates rich humus.
I stacked and screwed together the nominal chunks and printed
them (such as *Cant I* [*p.71*]).

Stacked wood at local nursery

Then, while experimenting with tree crosscuts, I discovered that the woodblock sections created an amazing impression. I wondered how oak would print, how ash would print, how cedar would print.

FINDING THE WOOD

I salvage dead or damaged logs from my property, the nearby nursery, local farms—pretty much anywhere. I could be driving on the highway and if there's a piece of wood on the side of the road, I often stop to take a closer look. Friends and those who know my work often will tell me about an unusual two-by-four or lead me to a fallen tree. Some of the wood comes to my studio that way. But usually when I'm out and about, if an intriguing cut grabs my attention, I'll want to print it. Like *Hemlock 82* [*p.28*], I hadn't seen those kinds of growth rings before, so I knew I had to do something with it. There's also my ongoing curiosity and desire to investigate species of trees that I haven't yet printed, or that I'm not familiar with. I'm always on the lookout for wood with different properties, densities, and textures.

THE BLOCK

When a tree comes to me or when I know a tree is being taken down, I'll cut up what I want, often looking for a specific area

Woodblocks for *Rolling Burl, Maple,* and *Pine Branch*

of investigation such as where the tree divides or branches intersect. And I'll keep cutting until I find something in the cross section that I think is engaging, until I have something I can work with. Usually, I make only a few cuts before I am satisfied with the block. Oftentimes, the cut itself reveals unexpected elements. In *Spruce* [*p. 31*], I discovered pruned branches and even a piece of metal embedded in the tree—I didn't know there was a piece of metal!

TOOLS

I work with a chain saw, hand planer, belt sander, palm sander, oxy-acetylene tanks, Bunsen burner, wire brush—and my hands. When printing, I always use my thumb and fingernail. Recently, I started to use a spoon. Also, a handmade, hornbeam brayer, and anything that's not going to rip the paper.

The studio is the most important tool that I have; it's my sanctuary.

Connecticut studio

PREPARING THE BLOCK
Sanding

After cutting the block, the next step is sanding. The goal is to sand the block as flat as possible, so that the paper doesn't crease when placed on the wood. In fact, the checked (cracked) version of *Southport Oak* [*p. 47*] was a challenge to print because the block's surface is so uneven. Once level, the block has shifted over time, expanding and contracting and producing hips and valleys and cracks that are a good quarter-inch from the printing surface. If I print it again, I may have to re-sand it.

Preparing block with belt sander

When sanding, I try to remove all the chain saw marks from the block (often, large cuts from the blade remain), because they will appear in the print. I want to achieve a very, very smooth surface. I can go from thirty-six-grit sandpaper to one hundred and fifty, sometimes two hundred (super fine)—all depending on the species of wood and how tight the grain is. *Cedar Pole* [*p. 51*], the very dense, two-hundred-year-old cedar, was sanded practically to a polish.

There have been times, however, that I have decided to keep some of the tooling marks in there (for instance, in *Ash* [*p. 21*] and *Maple Large* [*p. 56*]). To me, these marks add to the overall feeling of the print.

Burning and Sealing

Once I have a sanded surface, I burn it. Burning is a simple way to reduce the softer springwood, creating space between summerwood growth rings and distinguishing one ring from the next. At times, I've used a razor blade or Dremel tool to dig out the springwood, but that creates a very clean line that's too sterile for me.

After the burning, the wood is modeled. Depending on the softness of the wood, I use a wire brush, brass brush, or toothbrush to scrub the surface. For hardwood, I use a steel brush. But if the steel cuts into the summerwood, those brush marks might be visible

Sanding and burning the block for *Eastern Red Cedar*

Print set up for *Hemlock 82*

in the prints. It is important to pay attention to the species of the wood and which tools to use.

When the surface is finished to a degree that it will print well (or print the way I want it to print), I shellac it. Sealing it with an alcohol-based shellac protects the information on the block.

Creating a Platform

Finally, I prepare a platform for the block. For large pieces, this helps me move the block around the studio for printing or storage. The platform also provides a means of registration for the print— ensuring that the paper can be lifted and put down in the same location, whether for checking the print's progress, applying a color, or starting a new print in the edition.

PREPARING TO PRINT

Inking

Ink challenges me. I'm always learning about ink and viscosity— sometimes I use a stiff ink, sometimes I use a soft ink. I also like exploring various opacities—what works best for a particular piece of wood, for the species. Recently, I've been concentrating on printing some of the blocks with translucent ink first, then rolling and printing the same color but more opaque. This creates an especially strong impression of the summerwood. The print is not a fingerprint of the wood; it's not a stamp. It's the feel of the wood that I'm after.

Color adds a whole other dimension. *Red Ash* [*p.23*] is inviting and enticing. I love black and moss green, the colors that you see in the woods. I have also explored printing in multiple colors. *Spruce* is printed in black and brown, applied wet on wet. The finished piece has such a depth to it.

Paper

The paper itself is very important. I prefer to print on a thin paper, which allows me to see the piece emerging on the backside (I'm essentially seeing it backwards). Then, I can build the print, creating areas that are darker or lighter. Every time I lift up that paper, there is the risk of moving off register.

I also pay special attention to the orientation of the block on the paper. This is crucial—it's how the image is read. In some cases, I may vary the position of the block from one print to the next (see *Hemlock 82*, or for a more extreme example, *Pine I* and *Pine II* [*pp.60–61*]).

The reading of the print reveals another significant relationship. I retrieve something that grows up out of the ground, then I print a cross section, and hang it perpendicular to its growth. Usually, when I discover these trees, they are in woodpiles and they are horizontal. So, the print is my reality of seeing trees for materials.

PRINTING

Once the paper is down, I begin carefully pressing the rings. When I print, I'm trying to create an illusion of three dimensions— to get the block of wood to come alive on paper. I see the block in its physical form. If it printed totally flat, it would be boring. Depending on the image, black ink could be forward or back, white space could be forward or back. It's a dialog of push and pull.

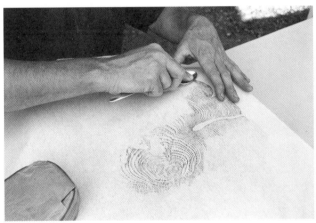

Inking the block and printing
(pressing the rings) of *Eastern
Red Cedar*

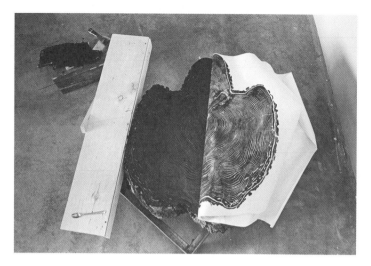

Block and print of *Hemlock 82*

Certain species of wood are much easier to print than others. Maple is one of the hardest to print, producing just the ghost of the growth rings. Also, depending on how a tree grows, the separation of springwood and summerwood rings will differ (for instance, favorable growth conditions result in looser rings, while dry or harsh conditions result in tight or erratic rings, which can be difficult to reproduce). Ash is a very responsive wood to print. It has a distinct separation of growth rings and information and textures transfer beautifully from block to paper. However, it would be unsatisfying to print ash all the time.

I constantly experiment. Lately, I've been printing on cotton cloth. It enables me to add and layer colors, and to use various turpentine oils and liquids to bleed the ink—which I haven't done on paper yet. I like the uncontrolled mark, that I can't predict the outcome. With *Pine I*, I printed the wood when it was still wet and the sap was oozing out. I wanted to see what would happen. A lot of the work is investigative. Sometimes I get a great print, but then I can't create it again. It's like a dance. It works or it doesn't. With *Ash*, every time I print it, it's different and engaging.

EDITIONS

I produce variable edition (VE) or artist variant (AV) prints.
In an edition of ten or fifteen, each print is produced from the
same block but there's a variation between the prints because they
are all hand printed. The block isn't going through the press,
it's not getting the same pressure, it's not completely flat. Many of
the woodblocks that I prepare to print wouldn't be press-ready.
It could be done but the prints wouldn't have those nuances, those
subtle differences.

Additionally, the block itself may change within the same
edition, showing noticeable variations. Sometimes a block still
has insects in it, so between prints a new hole will appear here
and there. Initially, when I printed *Ash*, the block didn't have any
cracks. Then it checked, and I printed the checked block. In the
winter, sitting on a heated floor, the wood dried out and the block
contracted, closing the check once again.

This is a characteristic of the material. Wood is always moving
because it consists of many open wood cells that are susceptible
to climate change. Unless hermetically sealed, there is essentially
no way to prevent it from cracking (especially a white or red oak).
I have started screwing plywood to the back of the blocks to try
to control the checking, as some will eventually break right apart.
But ultimately there's nothing wrong with that. The checks to
me are like another line. I don't see that as a negative. I see it as
a mark that is true to the material.

The more you work with one block of wood, the more you'll
know about how you want it to print. By the fifteenth print
of an edition, you've got it down. I'm not printing the edition
within a month, I'm printing it over years. To me, there's
something really nice about it not being over. It's like visiting
an old friend again.

BURLS

Working with burls is a recent endeavor. I've always collected burls.
I have carved into and made sculptures with burls (as well as some
bowls) but I had never thought of printing them. But why not?
I also like bookmatch burls, in which a cut is opened, like a book,
to reveal both sides in almost mirror image to each other.
(Bookmatching is a common practice in furniture and instrument
making.) The results are intriguing and point in a new direction
for my printmaking.

LOOKING FORWARD

I'd like to print species from all over the world, if I could.
My framer has access to the Charter Oak—the famous tree in
Connecticut (on the back of the state quarter) that was taken down
in a storm in the mid-1800s. He's going to bring me a limb or
a piece of the trunk or whatever he can, and I'll make a print of it.
To print a tree is another way of memorializing it. Perhaps I'm
in the business of memorializing trees.

One day, I'd love to print a whole tree. Not a massive tree.
I'd take the tree apart and recreate it. So far, I've concentrated on
the bole of trees. I'd like to print some roots. I haven't gone under
the ground yet. And I'd like to explore more bark, like the thick
(six-inch deep) cottonwood bark. The edge of the tree is a really
important part of the print for me: it's the beginning and the end.
And there are other surfaces to investigate and experiment with.
I'd also like to try new cuts—for instance, a diagonal cut rather
than a straight crosscut. Right now, it's endless.

Woodblock sculptures for *Picea Abies* (foreground) and *Spruce*

ACKNOWLEDGMENTS

Gina Kiss Gill, my beautiful bride, whose unconditional
love and understanding have given me the strength to be me.

Charles Fairchild Gill Jr. and Elizabeth Nash Muench
(Mom and Dad), for their endless support and for providing
me with the education, travel opportunities, and many
life lessons which have been so valuable to my development
as an artist.

Charles Fairchild Gill III, my brother, for all the fun we
continue to have together.

Megan Carey, my editor, for all her hard work and insight,
and for having the original idea to publish a book on
my work. Sara Bader, for her enthusiasm and the wonderful
studio photographs featured in this book. Deb Wood
and Paul Wagner, for their design and giving my work
a different life.

Phillip Fortune, for all his years of friendship and expertise
in photographing my work.

Steven Holmes, a great friend and curator, who continues
to help me see things in a different way.

Peter Hirschl, one of the best promoters and confidants
that anyone could have.

I would also like to thank all the galleries, museums,
collectors, family, and friends that have been so supportive
of my work over the years.

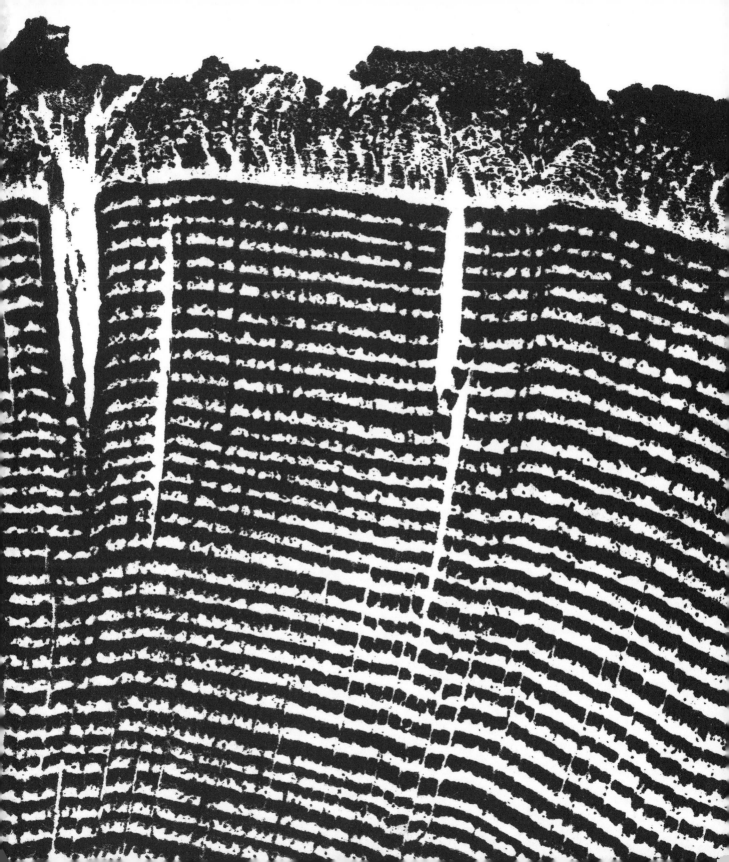